This journal belongs to:

_____

_____

_____

_____

Date:

Verse:

Thoughts & Notes:

Prayer Requests:

Date:

Verse:

Thoughts & Notes:

Prayer Requests:

Date:

Verse:

Thoughts & Notes:

Prayer Requests:

Date:

Verse:

Thoughts & Notes:

Prayer Requests:

Date:

Verse:

Thoughts & Notes:

Prayer Requests:

Date:

Verse:

Thoughts & Notes:

Prayer Requests:

Date:

Verse:

Thoughts & Notes:

Prayer Requests:

Date:

Verse:

Thoughts & Notes:

Prayer Requests:

Date:

Verse:

Thoughts & Notes:

Prayer Requests:

Date:

Verse:

Thoughts & Notes:

Prayer Requests:

Date:

Verse:

Thoughts & Notes:

Prayer Requests:

Date:

Verse:

Thoughts & Notes:

Prayer Requests:

Date:

Verse:

Thoughts & Notes:

Prayer Requests:

Date:

Verse:

Thoughts & Notes:

Prayer Requests:

Date:

Verse:

Thoughts & Notes:

Prayer Requests:

Date:

Verse:

Thoughts & Notes:

Prayer Requests:

Date:

Verse:

Thoughts & Notes:

Prayer Requests:

Date:

Verse:

Thoughts & Notes:

Prayer Requests:

Date:

Verse:

Thoughts & Notes:

Prayer Requests:

Date:

Verse:

Thoughts & Notes:

Prayer Requests:

Date:

Verse:

Thoughts & Notes:

Prayer Requests:

Date:

Verse:

Thoughts & Notes:

Prayer Requests:

Date:

Verse:

Thoughts & Notes:

Prayer Requests:

Date:

Verse:

Thoughts & Notes:

Prayer Requests:

Date:

Verse:

Thoughts & Notes:

Prayer Requests:

Date:

Verse:

Thoughts & Notes:

Prayer Requests:

Date:

Verse:

Thoughts & Notes:

Prayer Requests:

Date:

Verse:

Thoughts & Notes:

Prayer Requests:

Date:

Verse:

Thoughts & Notes:

Prayer Requests:

Date:

Verse:

Thoughts & Notes:

Prayer Requests:

Date:

Verse:

Thoughts & Notes:

Prayer Requests:

Date:

Verse:

Thoughts & Notes:

Prayer Requests:

Date:

Verse:

Thoughts & Notes:

Prayer Requests:

Date:

Verse:

Thoughts & Notes:

Prayer Requests:

Date:

Verse:

Thoughts & Notes:

Prayer Requests:

Date:

Verse:

Thoughts & Notes:

Prayer Requests:

Date:

Verse:

Thoughts & Notes:

Prayer Requests:

Date:

Verse:

Thoughts & Notes:

Prayer Requests:

Date:

Verse:

Thoughts & Notes:

Prayer Requests:

Date:

Verse:

Thoughts & Notes:

Prayer Requests:

Date:

Verse:

Thoughts & Notes:

Prayer Requests:

Date:

Verse:

Thoughts & Notes:

Prayer Requests:

Date:

Verse:

Thoughts & Notes:

Prayer Requests:

Date:

Verse:

Thoughts & Notes:

Prayer Requests:

Date:

Verse:

Thoughts & Notes:

Prayer Requests:

Date:

Verse:

Thoughts & Notes:

Prayer Requests:

Date:

Verse:

Thoughts & Notes:

Prayer Requests:

Date:

Verse:

Thoughts & Notes:

Prayer Requests:

Date:

Verse:

Thoughts & Notes:

Prayer Requests:

Date:

Verse:

Thoughts & Notes:

Prayer Requests:

Date:

Verse:

Thoughts & Notes:

Prayer Requests:

Date:

Verse:

Thoughts & Notes:

Prayer Requests:

Date:

Verse:

Thoughts & Notes:

Prayer Requests:

Date:

Verse:

Thoughts & Notes:

Prayer Requests:

Date:

Verse:

Thoughts & Notes:

Prayer Requests:

Date:

Verse:

Thoughts & Notes:

Prayer Requests:

Date:

Verse:

Thoughts & Notes:

Prayer Requests:

Date:

Verse:

Thoughts & Notes:

Prayer Requests:

Date:

Verse:

Thoughts & Notes:

Prayer Requests:

Date:

Verse:

Thoughts & Notes:

Prayer Requests:

Date:

Verse:

Thoughts & Notes:

Prayer Requests:

Date:

Verse:

Thoughts & Notes:

Prayer Requests:

Date:

Verse:

Thoughts & Notes:

Prayer Requests:

Date:

Verse:

Thoughts & Notes:

Prayer Requests:

Date:

Verse:

Thoughts & Notes:

Prayer Requests:

Date:

Verse:

Thoughts & Notes:

Prayer Requests:

Date:

Verse:

Thoughts & Notes:

Prayer Requests:

Date:

Verse:

Thoughts & Notes:

Prayer Requests:

Date:

Verse:

Thoughts & Notes:

Prayer Requests:

Date:

Verse:

Thoughts & Notes:

Prayer Requests:

Date:

Verse:

Thoughts & Notes:

Prayer Requests:

Date:

Verse:

Thoughts & Notes:

Prayer Requests:

Date:

Verse:

Thoughts & Notes:

Prayer Requests:

Date:

Verse:

Thoughts & Notes:

Prayer Requests:

Date:

Verse:

Thoughts & Notes:

Prayer Requests:

Date:

Verse:

Thoughts & Notes:

Prayer Requests:

Date:

Verse:

Thoughts & Notes:

Prayer Requests:

Date:

Verse:

Thoughts & Notes:

Prayer Requests:

Date:

Verse:

Thoughts & Notes:

Prayer Requests:

Date:

Verse:

Thoughts & Notes:

Prayer Requests:

Date:

Verse:

Thoughts & Notes:

Prayer Requests:

Date:

Verse:

Thoughts & Notes:

Prayer Requests:

Date:

Verse:

Thoughts & Notes:

Prayer Requests:

Date:

Verse:

Thoughts & Notes:

Prayer Requests:

Date:

Verse:

Thoughts & Notes:

Prayer Requests:

Date:

Verse:

Thoughts & Notes:

Prayer Requests:

Date:

Verse:

Thoughts & Notes:

Prayer Requests:

Date:

Verse:

Thoughts & Notes:

Prayer Requests:

Date:

Verse:

Thoughts & Notes:

Prayer Requests:

Date:

Verse:

Thoughts & Notes:

Prayer Requests:

Date:

Verse:

Thoughts & Notes:

Prayer Requests:

Date:

Verse:

Thoughts & Notes:

Prayer Requests:

Date:

Verse:

Thoughts & Notes:

Prayer Requests:

Date:

Verse:

Thoughts & Notes:

Prayer Requests:

Date:

Verse:

Thoughts & Notes:

Prayer Requests:

Date:

Verse:

Thoughts & Notes:

Prayer Requests:

Date:

Verse:

Thoughts & Notes:

Prayer Requests:

Date:

Verse:

Thoughts & Notes:

Prayer Requests:

Date:

Verse:

Thoughts & Notes:

Prayer Requests:

Date:

Verse:

Thoughts & Notes:

Prayer Requests:

Date:

Verse:

Thoughts & Notes:

Prayer Requests:

Date:

Verse:

Thoughts & Notes:

Prayer Requests:

Date:

Verse:

Thoughts & Notes:

Prayer Requests:

Date:

Verse:

Thoughts & Notes:

Prayer Requests:

Date:

Verse:

Thoughts & Notes:

Prayer Requests:

Date:

Verse:

Thoughts & Notes:

Prayer Requests:

Date:

Verse:

Thoughts & Notes:

Prayer Requests:

Date:

Verse:

Thoughts & Notes:

Prayer Requests:

Date:

Verse:

Thoughts & Notes:

Prayer Requests:

Date:

Verse:

Thoughts & Notes:

Prayer Requests:

Date:

Verse:

Thoughts & Notes:

Prayer Requests:

Date:

Verse:

Thoughts & Notes:

Prayer Requests:

Date:

Verse:

Thoughts & Notes:

Prayer Requests:

Date:

Verse:

Thoughts & Notes:

Prayer Requests:

Date:

Verse:

Thoughts & Notes:

Prayer Requests:

Date:

Verse:

Thoughts & Notes:

Prayer Requests:

Date:

Verse:

Thoughts & Notes:

Prayer Requests:

Date:

Verse:

Thoughts & Notes:

Prayer Requests:

Date:

Verse:

Thoughts & Notes:

Prayer Requests:

Date:

Verse:

Thoughts & Notes:

Prayer Requests:

Date:

Verse:

Thoughts & Notes:

Prayer Requests:

Date:

Verse:

Thoughts & Notes:

Prayer Requests:

Date:

Verse:

Thoughts & Notes:

Prayer Requests:

Date:

Verse:

Thoughts & Notes:

Prayer Requests:

Date:

Verse:

Thoughts & Notes:

Prayer Requests:

Date:

Verse:

Thoughts & Notes:

Prayer Requests:

Date:

Verse:

Thoughts & Notes:

Prayer Requests:

Date:

Verse:

Thoughts & Notes:

Prayer Requests:

Date:

Verse:

Thoughts & Notes:

Prayer Requests:

Date:

Verse:

Thoughts & Notes:

Prayer Requests:

Date:

Verse:

Thoughts & Notes:

Prayer Requests:

Date:

Verse:

Thoughts & Notes:

Prayer Requests:

Date:

Verse:

Thoughts & Notes:

Prayer Requests:

Date:

Verse:

Thoughts & Notes:

Prayer Requests:

Date:

Verse:

Thoughts & Notes:

Prayer Requests:

Date:

Verse:

Thoughts & Notes:

Prayer Requests:

Date:

Verse:

Thoughts & Notes:

Prayer Requests:

Date:

Verse:

Thoughts & Notes:

Prayer Requests:

Date:

Verse:

Thoughts & Notes:

Prayer Requests:

Date:

Verse:

Thoughts & Notes:

Prayer Requests:

Date:

Verse:

Thoughts & Notes:

Prayer Requests:

Date:

Verse:

Thoughts & Notes:

Prayer Requests:

Date:

Verse:

Thoughts & Notes:

Prayer Requests:

Date:

Verse:

Thoughts & Notes:

Prayer Requests:

Date:

Verse:

Thoughts & Notes:

Prayer Requests:

Date:

Verse:

Thoughts & Notes:

Prayer Requests:

Date:

Verse:

Thoughts & Notes:

Prayer Requests:

Date:

Verse:

Thoughts & Notes:

Prayer Requests:

Date:

Verse:

Thoughts & Notes:

Prayer Requests:

25746844R10084